How I Became A Fearless Woman
by Pamela Jansen

Dearest Kumari...
To such a precious girlfriend
whom I love so much.

Pammy P

This book is first and foremost dedicated to my Heavenly Father, for without Him I am nothing. To my mom Rosie, who has given of herself, even at the times when loving me and putting up with my frustrations, was such a difficult thing to endure, thank you mom. Was I worth it? In her eyes, yes, but at times it was, only in her eyes.

I thank my sister Marilyn, who decided to become a registered nurse after my accident. My big sister, who is so artistic and intelligent, helped me put this into the book format. She created three other books called the Amaryllis of Hawaii series. Thank you sistah, you rock.

To my OT mom, I called her that because to me, OT stood for an abbreviation of other mom. Actually, it was around the time I worked as an assistant Occupational Therapist and my OT mom, Mary Jo Griffin, opened her heart along with her home so that I would have a place to stay when I needed to be closer to my activities. She passed away on June 29, 2007. I love and miss you OT mom, Mary Jo Griffin, my mentor.

I thank all of my doctors; my orthopedic surgeons, Dr. Douglas Garland, Dr. Richard Feldman and Dr. Tye J. Ozounian, my neurologists, Dr. Fawaz Faisal, Dr. Frederick Amerongen, my internist, Dr. George Fischmann, my ear, nose and throat doctor, Dr. Warren Line, my dentists, Dr. David Farkas and Dr. Eric VanDuser, my obgyns, Dr. Brian Fenmore, Dr. Wayne Furr and Dr. Everett Wood, and my eye doctor, Dr. George Rajacich.

Thank you Fred Plessner, David Directo, Ila, Linda, Kip, Vanja and all the OT and Physical therapists at St. Joseph's Hospital Medical Center in Burbank, California.

Thanks also to Russell Lee Physical Therapy.

I thank my attorneys Ned Good and Barry Novack.

My photographer Mary Ann Halpin is the lady responsible for me being featured in the book, Fearless Women: Midlife Portraits by Nancy Alspaugh and Marilyn Kentz, photographed by Mary Ann Halpin. Thank you Mary Ann for believing in me. I love you dear.

*   *   *

FOREWORD

It is often said that life is not about the things that happen to you but instead the grace with which you handle them.

Pamela is an actress I met online, then in person, then cast in a movie. When I think of Pamela Jansen, I immediately think of two words: grace and fearlessness.

Grace because she is a model for all who struggle with any of life's unexpected challenges, no matter how large or small.

Fearlessness because of her willingness to charge into life's unknown adventures, fully aware that the experience of living is the ultimate gift.

Pamela's story is inspiring, her courage outstanding, despite the fact that on a night nearly 30 years ago, she wasn't expected to live through until morning. Her life changed forever.

Pamela never lets "what happened" define her, she has defined herself! She is the blonde who raises cane and I can't imagine a more delightful storyteller to spend some time with.

Enjoy the gift that is this book by Pamela Jansen. Consider yourself blessed for having had the opportunity to get to know her a little better. Remember that every day is a gift. And know that everything that "happens" in life is an opportunity to display your own fearless grace.

Foreword by Bonnie Gillespie
Cricket Feet Casting
Hollywood, California 2007

INTRODUCTION

This is my story about how I learned to overcome the effects of a traumatic brain injury, after my devastating car accident. I am just the average woman, who ran into misfortune. It could have happened to any one.

We all have a choice though, when something of this nature happens. To just exist, or to pick up and live a full life, by learning how to deal with limitations. I chose the latter.

My intentions in writing this are that I wanted to share, not just with accident victims, but also with the person who has lost any hope to see that change is possible. I am referring to the change in our outlook on ourselves. We must love ourselves. I believe that is where inner peace and healing begin. I grew up figure skating, until I eventually trained to enter Ice Capades. I remember performing on the ice at the Los Angeles Forum, while auditioning. It was so smooth I felt as if I was gliding on glass.

The reactions of the panel were that my skating was good, but my thighs were too big. They went on to say that, with constant travel between shows, there'd be no time to repair costumes if the seams were split. Since I was young and had no thoughts regarding limitation of time, my reaction to their decision was. *I've practiced long enough and now they want more? I don't think so.* I was disappointed but not distraught. I will say though, that that similar determination to work for something, would come in handy at a later point of this one's life.

Years later I was an instructor for Jack La Lannes Health Spa. Guess what? No more heavy thighs! It was not the kind of job with a future though. Later on, I was hired as a prop maker for Warner Bros. Studios. I worked on such shows as Wonder Woman, Fantasy Island, Eight Is Enough... I also took jobs on my own, designing and constructing stained glass windows.

A certain night, December 6th, 1978 on my way home from work, I was broad sided by a truck, and fell into a coma.

I awoke sometime in January 1979, but it still took me an additional 5 weeks to regain awareness. Now that I am awake, I haven't stopped.

Hurdle after hurdle might have slowed me down temporarily, but I knew there was a reason that I was still here. I even attempted to return to my old job at the studios, but was unable to keep up. Another hurdle.

I knew for a fact that God allowed me to remain here on earth, but there were times when the reasons seemed very cloudy. I also knew that everyone of us had struggles of some sort or another, but life had become very challenging for me.

Say that you've been striving very hard for something and you are just beginning to see the fruits. Suddenly, there's this feeling of insignificance trying to tell you to just give up, that you will never achieve. Don't listen.

All of us have that weak inner self that is so much against our succeeding because it is scared and until we learn to recognize that voice, it has won.

I enrolled in Bible College sometime around August of 1985 and graduated in May of 1989. During those years, I came to realize that it's okay to be different, because, I am enough. That, friends who couldn't look past my imperfections and see my heart, well they were not the kind of friends that I needed. Once again, my goals in writing this book are not only to share my story with accident victims, but also for the person who has not experienced a physical loss, yet they are struggling emotionally.

Ever since the day I began sharing my story with people, it was if I had been buttered up and frosted like an angel food cake. No one wanted to see me hurt any more than I had been already. To them Pam was such an example of courage.

What had yet to be witnessed though, was the anger inside, pushed down so deep that even I was not about to confront it. I was furious that this happened. Why me? Why not me was the question I had to accept. The realization would not arrive overnight. I speak to different groups about my story and how to never lose hope, or they will give in to that fear of defeat.

Acting became a love of mine that I am not about to shake. I began studying in 2001 because I realized, if I can't get there behind the camera, I'll get there in front!

This isn't intended to be a self help book, as I am just sharing my experiences and how I myself endured them. Then again, if it helps you in any way, then more power to you.

The time was around 11:00 p.m., when I turned onto my street. My house was a block down past the stop sign. I was planning on walking in the front door and heading directly to my bed, because I needed to be at the studios at 6:00 a.m..

I approached the stop sign and unable to view oncoming traffic due to overgrown hedges, I edged out. Along came a pickup truck, traveling at an estimated rate of fifty miles per hour. I was broad sided by that truck. Later on I was told that the truck left fifty six feet of skid marks and pushed my car another ten feet.

Since the accident was only a block from my house, mom heard the whole thing. With a mother's intuition, my mom instantly arose and she ran down the street. There it was, my red Pinto. She ran to the car and there I was, shoved under the glove compartment.

As it turned out, the yard that my car was pushed into, was the house of the parents of a paramedic, who had by chance been visiting them at that moment.The paramedic, Jack Barber, saved my life. He was off duty when he ran outside after hearing the crash. I was told that he lifted my chin to open my airway, as my mangled body laid waiting for the ambulance to arrive.

I had been thrown across the inside of the car, pushed over the stick shift and the back of my head smashed into a broken door handle.

That was the night I left my former life behind.

SECTION ONE

It's the wee early hours of the morning and the sun is beginning to peek over the hills. The Hollywood sign is becoming visible. It's a bit chilly, but I don't care, to be working on the show "Wonder Woman" is enough to get me motivated.

Heading towards the stage, rubbing my hands together as I blow on them to keep warm, I step inside. The stage where the show will be filmed, starts out as a hollowed out building and becomes a lifelike creation of whatever it's meant to be.

I am looking around at the beginning of a project, full of workers, building different structures. Some of the guys have a cigarette in one hand and a hammer in the other. When they proceed to set a nail in, they hold the butt with the edge of their lip.

The foreman is already assigning jobs to the workers, so I walk up to him, leaning over to read his name,

"Hi Dave."

"Hi Pam," he's glancing at his clipboard, "ready to go? You'll be working with Steve over there."

"The guy with the red hair?" I say as I'm walking over to find my partner.

"Hi Steve, I'm Pam. Where should I start?"
He's giving me the once over, looking like he approves.

"Hi Pam, so you're my partner for today. My my, it's gonna be rough."

"Please Steve, don't make me stand out any more than I already do."

"OK partner, first we need to build these door frames." He held up the prints.

"I'll go gather supplies."

"What should I do Steve? I can't be standing around."

Too late, he didn't even hear me, now what? I'll just try to appear as if I'm studying these prints, even though they're totally Greek to me. I wonder if anyone notices. Steve walks up with the wood, so I anxiously pull him aside.

"You understand don't you? I just don't want to stand out and be looked at."

"Don't worry Pam, it will happen. You won't be just one of the guys, but they'll get used to having you around. Now come on, look the part."

Work is going smooth, although I sure am following him around a lot.

"Lunch," the foreman yells.

"Hey Pam can I buy you lunch?"

"Thanks anyway Steve, but then I wouldn't be just one of the guys."

I actually wanted to do some star searching on my lunch break.

It is such a gorgeous day and what an exciting place to be for work. Tattoo, from Fantasy Island passes me and I wave hi. *OK, so I'm still star searching. Cafeteria food there in that exciting atmosphere was a treat. Time to get back, wonder who else I'll see.*

I continue walking towards the set, when I turn the corner and oh my God, John Travolta looks at me and smiles, "Hi."

"Hi," I'm just trying to keep my composure. The adrenaline is pumping. *I am definitely going to enjoy this place and getting paid to be here.*

Back on the set, Steve is already setting up for our next project.

"Hi Steve, what are we doing now?"
He's trying to decide where to put me, I can tell.

"I need you to measure and cut these 2x's, then lay them out on these marks."

"Steve, let me hammer, please?"

"OK Pam, but make sure to hit the nail on the head, because the camera picks up elephant tracks."
I look at him, "Huh?"

"Elephant tracks are the marks that the hammer makes when you miss the nail." He begins to measure, cut the wood and lay it on the floor. With a big smile, hammer in hand, I say,

"OK, step aside." I hold up a nail. "16 penny?" I look at Steve and he nods his head.

After about ten whacks, I look up to see a bunch of guys laughing at the nail beginning to lean. *What I miss is the foreman walking by and rolling his eyes.*

It's been a long day and trying to blend in isn't going as I planned.

"Quittin' time," the foreman yelled while fanning through some yellow slips.

"Uh oh Pam, know what those are?" Steve said,

"They're layoff slips."

The boss walks up and hands me one. I'm puzzled.

"You might just get picked up on another show," Steve said, "this is a funny business."

Sure enough, in the mill, there's a note on the bulletin board with my name, instructing me to show up at stage 16 and report to Bruce.

* * *

DECEMBER 6, 1978

Months have passed and I am keeping up with the guys now.

"Quiet on the set," yells the director, "Action."

There are people around for every job necessary to make a movie. The producer, director, lighting, make up artists, cameramen and actors surround the set.

"OK that's a wrap," yells the director.

It's the end of the day and I am sitting on my Stingray bike, walking it to the gate, when I hear someone calling my name. I turned around to see my old partner Steve. He catches up,

"Hey cutie, are you cruising?"

"Hi Steve, cruising, what's that?"

"How many swings does it take you to drive a 16 penny with no elephant tracks?"

"Seven, on a good day," I said.

He put his hand on my shoulder, which made me a bit uncomfortable.

"Done for the day? Let's grab a bite."

I was thankful that I had a legitimate excuse, because even though Steve was a very nice person, he wasn't my type.

"I'll have to say no because, I need to go to my other job and install a window that I made, but thanks Steve."

"OK, I'll see you tomorrow," he said.

My other job is a layout of stained glass windows, I am designing and making for a house that is under construction.

* * *

Later that night.

Man this window turned out to be much better than what I expected.

"Hey Mike," I yelled down the stairs, "Would you help me install this?"

"It's so late Pam. I need to get home. Can you wait until tomorrow?"

"Please Mike, I've waited long enough to see this puppy in place. Come up and look at it. I want you to see why you hired me. You're gonna want to see it installed too."

Hesitantly, he staggered up the steps and stood before my workbench.

"Nice job Pam. Keep this up and you're really going to go places. OK, how do we go about this?"

"OK, we're going to slide this halfway off the bench and then start tipping it, until the window is straight up." He is nodding his head.

"Then we'll place it in the opening, with the rebar supports on the outside."

We put the window in and I just stood there, noticing how attention to detailing the window had really paid off. I was one pleased cookie.

*   *   *

Long Roses window

IRIS OCTAGON BEVELED GLASS WINDOW

A WORK IN PROGRESS

OCTAGON WINDOW INSTALLED IN 1978

ME AT MY STAINED GLASS JOB

10:30 p.m.

"Gotta run now, see you tomorrow after work."

It was late, but I wanted to stop and tell my friend Dede, about my job promotion I received today. I now have a #1 card in Local 44 at the studios.

AT THE BAR

"Pam, let's have a drink to celebrate."

"No thanks Dede, I have to work tomorrow. Can I give you a ride home?"

"Would you? I'm supposed to wait for John, but it's late."

We pulled into her driveway,

"Pam," Dede's laughing "there's no door handle."

"I know, it broke off one day," I told her. The stump of the handle was all that remained.

"I'll open it, from the outside." I was laughing as I walked around to open her door.

"Your destination, madam."

"Pam, it's late so, why don't you just stay here?"

"No thanks, I have to punch in at 6:00am tomorrow, and I need fresh clothes. I'll see you later."

"OK, thanks Pam."

I then set off on the ten minute drive home, that in a flash, became a three month journey.

* * *

SECTION TWO

Approaching the final corner, that I was to encounter before reaching my house, was a stop sign, but bushes blocked the view of oncoming traffic. Sitting at that stop sign, I was picturing my newly completed window and thinking about my job promotion I had received just today.

I edged out and in a split second, the truck broad sided me. My brain had bounced inside of my skull and all of the nerves coming out of the spine into the brain stem were bent like a flower stem.

At the moment of the accident, back at the house, which was half of a block down from the tragedy, mom was watching a movie on TV. The scene location was of some hospital grounds. They were the grounds of the hospital, where I'd be arriving within a matter of minutes.

Just then, mom heard the noise of a loud screech, that ended with the sound of a crash. A mother's intuition kicked in.

"Oh no," she began to run to the corner. There was my red Pinto. Driver side, smashed in, but where was I? She rushed over, to find me and there I lay, rolled up and shoved beneath the glove compartment.

MY PINTO AFTER THE CRASH

The paramedic, whose yard my car had been pushed into, ran out, hurried over to my unconscious body and began to help. He gently lifted my chin to open my airway. Mom grabbed his arm, "Is she alive?"

"So far," he said without taking his eyes off of me. "I'm a paramedic. I'll stay with her until the ambulance comes. Someone called for one, right?"

By this time, neighbors had gathered around and since it was late, most of them were wearing pajamas. A man in a checkered bathrobe raised his hand and said, "I did." Mom just nodded her head to him.

While they waited for the ambulance to arrive, mom was somewhat able to carry on a conversation. Looking down towards the paramedic who was on his knees, helping Pam, mom's voiced cracked and she took a deep breath trying to form the words, "I've never seen you before. Where do you live?"

Still, without taking his eyes off me, he said, "I live in another town, but my parents live over there," He pointed to the yard where my car had been pushed into, "I just dropped by to visit them tonight."
Tears rushed down mom's cheeks, "Oh thank God."

After about twenty minutes, the ambulance arrived. Mom was hysterical by then when she screamed, "Get my daughter out!"

They free my twisted body from the car and place me on a stretcher.

"Take her to St. Joseph's!" mom screamed.

"Sorry ma'am," one of the paramedics explained, "but we're instructed to take her to the nearest facility." Mom climbed into the ambulance to sit beside my limp body and they raced off. Minutes later, they pulled up to the emergency room at Serra Memorial in Sun Valley.

Mom jumped out and ran in to call dad. He was at a restaurant with some clients.

"Jim, Pam's been in an accident! Come to Serra Memorial hospital!" she screamed. In shock he replies, "I'll be right there." Mom had already hung up the phone.

Upon arriving, dad took the elevator up to the second floor. There were people walking around the halls, some in whites, others in plain clothes, some in business suits, but you could tell which were the people visiting sick ones, because they just had this look of concern, maybe of uncertainty.

Dad continued down the hall, passing some tearful people, some joyful ones, when suddenly he saw mom standing and listening to a Doctor speak to her. Mom's eyes were dark and swollen. The Doctor has told her that I have taken a severe jolt to the head.

Dad walks up and the Doctor continues, "We'll need to perform numerous tests to assess the damage your daughter has sustained. As it looks now, we do not expect her to survive the night."

Mom is sobbing uncontrollably. That first night, mom and dad sat alongside my bed.

The calendar on the wall read December 6, 1978.

DECEMBER 7, 1978.

It was a long night but it's dawn now and I am breathing on my own. A different doctor came into the room, and stood at the foot of my bed, examining my chart. I am still sound asleep. The doctor then looked up from the chart, over to mom and dad and said, "Hello, I'm Doctor White. I'll be the attending physician for today."
Mom looked at him and with hopes of a good report she said, "Hi, we're Pam's parents. I'm Rosie and this is Jim."

Dad shakes his hand, "Hello, what can you tell me about my daughter?"

"Well," the Doctor begins, "the fact that she has survived the night is a good sign. A CAT Scan determined signs of brain stem and cerebella damage, along with a cerebral contusion. We're going to continue monitoring her and wait."

Dad holds mom in his arms, as tears stream down her face.

"Jimmy, what are we going to do?"
He squeezes her extra firmly and says,

"Pammy's tough, we have to wait."
Mom gasps, "Jim you need to call Marilyn!"

Looking so hesitant, dad says, "I'll call, but how should I say it? Marilyn, Pammy's been in an accident and they don't even know if she's going to live?" He choked up.

24

On dad's way out, walking down the halls, once again were the same scenes he saw while walking in. People everywhere, in different clothing, for different reasons. Jovial faces, serious faces, some very serious.

This time though, I guess since it was morning, there were kids running around. He thought of Pammy when she was just a little girl.

Dad arrived home and just sat on the couch reminiscing. In his thoughts, Marilyn and Pam are young girls, seven and five years old. All of a sudden, Pam runs in through the kitchen, from the pool.

"Pammy, watch it, you're going to slip."
The stillness in the house came every year when the girls went off to summer camp, but always with the expectation of return.

MARILYN & PAMMY IN STRAW CHAIR AT THE VINELAND POOL

Reality is back and he longs for those moments to return, as he hesitantly reaches for the phone. Marilyn is living up in Oakland. She was soldering a stained glass window when the phone rang. Dad is bewildered trying to find the right words to say, but then again are there any right words? He took a deep breath and sighed.

The conversation went just as dad had expected, with Marilyn hanging up to make arrangements to be there that evening. Dad had said, "Marilyn, Pam's been in an accident." He tearfully continued, "They don't know if she'll make it. I, I don't know if she'll still be alive when you get here."

DECEMBER 7, 1978. Evening

Marilyn flew home and dad was there to pick her up. He was so pale and choked up. They drove straight to the hospital, where upon arrival, Marilyn jumped out of the car and ran in. She saw mom, sitting in silence beside my bed, and ran up to her. There were no words, just tears.

*   *   *

As the days passed, there was little change as I lay there, sound asleep.

DECEMBER 24, 1978 - CHRISTMAS EVE

Two and a half weeks after the accident and I am still, sound asleep. Mom and dad were given small amounts of hope for recovery. Then it happened.

Mom and dad were sitting on chairs, at the foot of my bed and in tears of exhaustion, mom turned to dad and said,

"It's been 18 days. What are we supposed to do?"

Dad is trying to give her hope, but at the same time, he is exhausted. Then he comes up with one of his humorous replies, "Hey Rosie, you carried Pam in your tummy for five extra weeks. Remember, she was five weeks over-due?"

Marilyn walked up to me and leaned over the bed rail, took my hand and began to sing a song by Nicolette Larson. "It's gonna take a lot of love to make this work out fine." Then Marilyn grabbed my hand and yelled, "Pam wake up, it's Christmas Eve and we have to finish our shopping!" At that, I opened one eye. Marilyn screamed again,

"Look she's waking up!"

My parents jumped up to see. I was told that my eye stayed open for approximately ten seconds, then closed. Marilyn told me to hold her hand, but I did nothing. In fact, with no expression, I lay there for ten seconds then closed my eye and drifted back into a coma. Dad disappeared into the hallway and eventually returned with the Doctor at his side. Doctor Brown touched me to see if there was any response. Nothing. Mom was ecstatic though. "Doctor, you should've seen her a minute ago. Her eye was staring straight ahead."

He showed a minimal amount of excitement while taking my blood pressure.

Still trying to head off any misleading hopes while whisking through the pages of my chart, he focuses on my still body and remarks,

"This is a positive sign, so I will be upgrading her prognosis, which will now stand at a 60/40 percent chance of waking up. She most likely will never walk or talk again."

To that, with tears rushing down her face, mom exclaimed,

"You don't know my daughter."

* * *

JANUARY 1979

Day after day, I just lay there. My family was waiting in anxious expectation for another sign.

It is now morning and I am still unconscious, but as my mom walked into the room, my right leg is sliding back and forth on the sheets.

"Pam!" she screamed. She ran to get the doctor, who approached my bedside, put his hand on my arm and said, "Pam. Pam, look at me." Nothing. No response.

"Overall," the Doctor said, "this is enough of a sign. I'll be making arrangements for her transfer to Rancho Los Amigos."

"But Doctor," mom said, "we've already applied and she was turned down, remember?"

"I know, that's because they only accept patients who exhibit slight signs of recovery.

Since the initial application she has shown remarkable improvement. Don't worry, she'll be accepted now." After the necessary paperwork, it was confirmed.

Pam is in!

*   *   *

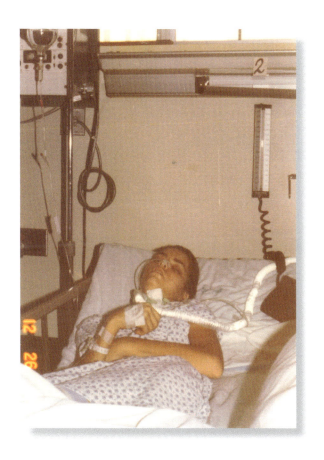

PAM STILL IN COMA 20 DAYS LATER.

SECTION THREE

JANUARY 1979.

The ambulance arrived to transport me to Rancho Los Amigos Hospital in Downey, California. Even though I was still unconscious, I have shown slight signs of recovery.

During the drive on the freeway, mom notices that my eyes are staring out the ambulance window. "Pam, what are you looking at?" No response, but there's one of those slight signs, both eyes are open.

Entering the Head Trauma ward at Rancho Los Amigos, is like stepping into a realm of life that has been set apart from everyday existence. People don't stop to think about a place like this, but if they did, I'm sure they would develop a down to earth gratitude.

The ward consists of patients who have been involved in severe accidents. Nearly every patient had a shaved head, although I didn't because I had a closed head injury.

Almost all of the patients were confined to wheelchairs. Most of the young men had a run in with a motorcycle, the women an automobile. Some had been in fights and hit in the head. Needless to say, it was a busy place.

I am still semi-comatose at this point, but gradually waking up, after all, that was the reason for my being accepted into Rancho Los Amigos, because I am beginning to show signs of progression. The paramedics signed me in at the front desk and then left. Dorothy, the head nurse on that ward takes me to my room and prepares me for bed.

Coming out of my coma was a slow, gradual process.

As the initial CAT Scan determined, I sustained a cerebral contusion along with a brain stem injury. All motor activity is created in the Cerebrum, which is the largest portion of the brain. The smallest portion, located on the back of the brain, near the bottom is the Cerebellum. This is where speech, balance and motor control are fine tuned. My head had smashed into the door and bruised my brain.

Injury to one side of the brain affects the opposite side of the body and I had what is called a contra coup injury, where the brain bounces inside the skull, causing damage to both sides of the body. The major impact was on the right, causing the complete left side of my body to retain the damage. The brain stem injury bent all the cranial nerves in half "like a flower stem" causing multiple problems, some still with me today.

There I was, at 21 years old, wearing diapers, fed meals through a tube inserted into my nostril, a tracheotomy that overflowed often, drooling 90% of the time. I wasn't able to communicate the sensation of severe pain. I was unable to move the left side of my body and had no voice.

But that's just a taste of the mercy of God. He was about to bring me through the adventure of my life, a route that in my wildest dreams I could not have imagined, but there's God cleaning up the mess once again.

It is still January 1979. I am alone now, lying in bed, but this time awake enough to think. *Where am I? What's happening? Why can't I talk?*

All of a sudden this white cloud is forming at my bedside. *Why is everything turning white? My hand and fingers won't move. Why?* There's a body taking form beside my bed. It's Jesus Christ. *I know You.* He was standing so serene and peaceful. I felt so comforted.

Will You say something to me? Why can't I speak? My mouth isn't moving, but I know You know what I'm saying.

My eyes are focused on His. I am communicating through my thoughts, with my eyes focused on Him.

Where am I? Every part of my body is so tight that I hurt so bad. My arm, my leg, why can't I move them? Jesus, what's happening? The Vision then disappeared.

*   *   *

The sun has risen now, and two therapists enter the room. I am looking over at them, saying to them, but without moving my face or making a sound, *Who are you? Where am I? Why can't I talk? Help me.*

One of the ladies, a beautiful Blonde, leans over the bed railing,

"Good morning, Pam, my name is Sandy and I'll be your physical therapist while you're here at Rancho. Keep those eyes open Pam."

Sandy has her hand on my cheek, turning my face toward them. She continues, "Pam, this is B.J., she'll also be working with you. Can you look at her?"

Who are you?

"She's definitely watching me, Sandy." B.J. said. I lay there staring at them and thinking, *Why can't you hear me? I am talking to you. My voice, why can't I talk? I feel like I'm screaming and nothing is coming out. No sound at all. Nobody will listen to me.*

"Now Pam, I need to test your range of motion." Sandy reaches for my right arm, "I'll be lifting your arms and legs to see how far you can stretch."

Ouch, you're killing me. Quit pulling on my arm. B.J. is once again in my face. "Pam, we're gonna sit you up and see how you do with balance." B.J. continued, "Now hang onto the bed rails, they're one of your favorite things."

Both of them lift my shoulders, supporting my back until I'm sitting up. I am like an infant, who is unable to sit up without being held onto, with my chin resting on my chest.

"Pam," Sandy said, "you're going to have to hold that head up if you want to balance yourself."

They let go while holding their arms toward me. There isn't a moment of hesitation as I fall over on my left side.

"Whoops, timber." B.J. said, "At least we know where to begin therapy. It's break time, we'll work some more after lunch."

* * *

All right, a break. Come on, why are you tying my hands to the railing again? Where am I gonna go? Why won't you look at me? Where's my voice? This isn't fair.

They leave and once again, I am lying here, not knowing where I am, or how I got here. *This looks like a hospital room, so why am I here? This is the strangest dream I've ever had. Those plants and flowers on the shelf are all so pretty. It's too bad when I wake up that, they'll all be gone. I'd really like to wake up now.*

I have fallen off into a deeper sleep and now I am on a mountain top which stretches a quarter of a mile in diameter. There is such an aura of loneliness. It's as if I am the only person around. The location is somewhere out of state, far far away from my home. It feels so strange because there is no one else yet in the dream.

I am here to meet my boyfriend who shows up with another woman at his side, letting me know that we are no longer together, and that I should leave. These blue and green elephant heads are floating by me laughing and breathing fire.

I had never seen them before and so I screamed, Who are you? Get away!

Now in the dream are just my father and I. We are rowing in a canoe at night. It's dark outside, the only light is from a full moon. We are not speaking and so the only sound you can hear is of the thousands of crickets. My father leans forward to push me out. I am gasping for air, holding my stomach to comfort a pain deep inside. I am completely defenseless, but I never fall into the water. The fear just drifts on.

* * *

Later that afternoon.

Sandy peeks her head in the doorway and says, "Hey Pam, time to wake up and get to work." *Ah, come on. Already? I'm taking a nap.*

"Pam, look at me." Sandy says, "You've been chosen for something special. You're going to be a movie star for us. We'll be filming your progress from the beginning. Isn't that exciting? This is Carl. He'll be the camera man." *If you could only hear me, you'd know how exciting this is.*

"OK Pam," B.J. is standing behind a wheelchair, "here's your taxi."
Sandy comes around to help.

"Pam, you have to let go of the railing so we can get you out of bed. Now, try to help us by moving your right leg to the side. I'll move the other one, for now that is."

Then we can put you in the chair." They sit me up and Sandy gently pulls my right leg off of the bed, then my left.

"OK Pam," BJ pushes my wheelchair up to my bed.

The hallway is filled with patients, in wheelchairs, parked along the wall. This is the Head Trauma ward, meaning for patients who have sustained traumatic head injuries. Nearly every patient is non responsive and is wheelchair bound.

This place is crowded beyond belief. Everyone is sitting down, some are being wheeled in different directions, while others are just hanging out, but no one is smiling. Can't anyone even smile? Where are we going now? This dream is too dull. I really, really want to wake up.

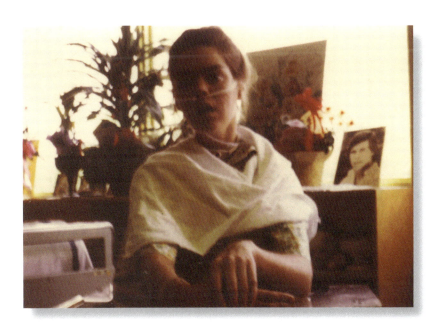

We entered the gym, filled with more patients in wheelchairs.

"Now Pam," Sandy said, "this is the tilt table. We're going to work with it daily. Please honey, try to hold that head up. OK, first of all, you'll be lying on it, and we'll fasten the straps to secure you to the table, then B.J. will push a button and guess what, you'll be standing up."

I just really want to go back to bed. Why are you tying my arms down?

All of a sudden, the table begins slanting.

Oh my God, my leg, what's happening? Those blue and green elephant heads are floating in front of me again, laughing and breathing fire. Who are you? Help! Let me down. Help me please. I can't stand it. My tracheotomy gasps for breath, Hhhhh. Get away from me, quit laughing. I hurt so bad! God. I just wanna go back to bed.

Another therapist walks nearby. My hands are loosely tied to the table and so I grab for her hair only to rip her wig off. My fingers were locked around the wig and they had to pry my hand open, to get it back. Elsie, maintained her composure and put the wig back on.

You could tell that, everyone in the room, who was alert enough, wanted to crack up, but out of respect, they refrained. Although as soon as Elsie chuckled, the room broke into hysterics.

There, now she'll listen.

Sandy, while trying to maintain her composure, lowers the table and unstraps me, "We're going to let you go back to bed now."

All right, bed. Why is it that I feel so safe in bed? Nobody can hurt me there. I have time to figure out where I am, and why I'm here.

Days had passed, and a Catholic priest is now moving from bed to bed visiting with patients in the Intensive Care Ward. He glances at the chart on the foot of my bed, then stands at my bedside and says,

"Hello Pamela."

At that, I roll over and raise my third finger at him.

"That's quite all right dear, you're not responsible. Bless you my child."

At that point I was still unable to vocalize anger, but my third finger did excessively.

FEBRUARY 17, 1979

I am sitting outside in the hospital yard in my wheelchair, enjoying the soft morning sunlight. Two men are walking towards me. *Who are these guys, I wondered. They look familiar. I looked again, then realized, it's my boss Bruce and Bob from the studios. Bruce has a tool belt, the kind I wore at the studios. They're here to take me to work. OK, I really, really need to wake up now.*

When Bruce gets close enough, he holds up the tool belt. "OK Jansen, break's over." He laughed as he hugged me.

They are both sitting Indian style on the grass beside my wheelchair. I am still unable to speak at this point, and so everything is in my thought realm. They understood by keeping the conversation moving and making me smile with half of my face. I'd try to move my left cheek, but that side of my body was still atrophied. Uh oh, here comes Sandy.

"OK Pam, break is over," she said. Bruce chuckles, recalling the same words when greeting me. Sandy unlocked my wheels and turned me toward the torture chamber.

"We'll see you again, Pam." Bruce and Bob waved goodbye.

But wait guys, aren't we going to work?

* * *

FEBRUARY 19, 1979

One morning after a hearing test, I was with Sandy in Physical Therapy. She had me working on the sit down bicycle.

"OK Pam," she said, "I'm going to support your legs as you peddle. Pam, pick that head up."

I am staring at the floor, my chin resting on my chest and my eyes are fixed toward the floor.

My mom and sister were there also, when suddenly I looked up at them and said,

"WHAT HAPPENED TO ME? WHERE AM I?"

Tears filled both Mom's and Marilyn's eyes as they screamed, "Pam".

Sandy is smiling from ear to ear, as her eyes are focused on me and says, "Welcome back Pamela."

Mom is just ecstatic and Marilyn is thrilled. Finally, I've come back. Some others that were in the room shared in the excitement by giving a thumbs up, then turning back to their own patients.

They excitedly transfer me to my wheelchair and rush me back to my room so they could explain the situation to me. When they got me back in bed they told me,

"Pam you had a car accident and you were in a coma for 5 weeks. You woke up around a month ago, but never said a thing, until now. Oh Pam..." Tears were falling from mom's eyes as she spoke. I responded to my mom, "You smell like cigarettes." She was a little embarrassed in front of Sandy. I then turned to my sister and said, "You smell like rotten sour cream." She had just finished a bag of sour cream onion potato chips and my mom had just smoked a cigarette. They didn't really care what I said because they were just so happy. The sign of my being able to smell, was the initial sign that I was on my way back because my sensory perception was intact.

They can finally hear me. Is this it? I'm awake, but I'm still in the same place. How come I hurt so bad? This was real the whole time. I wasn't dreaming. Those ugly elephant heads were real.

41

Later, dad walks in to the moment that both himself and mom have been waiting for since the accident on December 6th. Tears filled his eyes when, he walked up to me and said, "Hi Pammy," he leaned over and hugged me. I recognize him immediately, "Hi dad," and since my mind was consumed by the need for details, "the guy that hit me, was he sorry?"

Mom and dad glanced at each other, and dad is re-calling a time when, two weeks after the accident, I am laying in a coma, with them not aware of even a chance of my ever waking up. The man whose truck hit my Pinto, knocked on their front door and proceeded to ask them for their insurance information so that he could get his truck fixed. Dad tried to remain professional and not show the emotion of rage he was holding towards the guy.

Then dad remembered what a neighbor had told him regarding the man's reaction, after his truck had hit me. The neighbor told my dad that, the man got out of his truck, walked up to their house and showing little emo-tion, said something like,

"I don't want to be arrested for a hit and run, so can I use your phone?"

* * *

Back at Rancho, Sandy walks into the room and seeing that we were done talking, she says,

"OK Pam, it's time to get back to work."

She put me in the wheelchair and whisked me off. Mom and dad went for coffee, because mom couldn't stand to watch me in so much pain.

Oh boy, I now have a voice that they can hear.

"Now honey," Sandy is busy arranging me, "we're go ing to place your right leg in this sling, to concentrate on strengthening the left side of your body."

I was already screaming.

Sandy said, "Pam we haven't even started yet. I still need to put the sling in place."

It feels as if a carving knife has been inserted into the left side of my pelvis. With my right hand tied down, my right leg in the air, the left leg is holding all of my weight up.

"Ouch, damn it, let me down! I can't stand it," I screamed.

The screaming is so loud, that a washcloth is stuffed into my mouth. My right hand was already tied down and the left hand won't move, so I was essentially bound and gagged. Most of the other patients were not at an alert stage, as of yet, so it didn't really matter. There was this one patient though. His name was Gus. He just sat there in his wheelchair, laughing as he was enjoying the show. Here come those elephant heads again, floating by, laughing and breathing fire.

When is this going to stop?

FEBRUARY 25, 1979

Mom took me to Mass today and I lasted the entire time. I am still not completely awake though. I got mad at her and she slapped my hand because I dug my nails in her's. Then she asked me if I knew why she slapped me. I said yes, you slimy whore.

FEBRUARY 26, 1979

I pulled out my naso-gastric tube again. That's the tube that I am fed my meals through my nose. Lynn, the nurse, was inserting into my nostril when I told her to,

"Get your f---king hands off my head."

Mom said to me, "Pam, your father and I were warned about these spurts of anger, but the language you're using is too much for me."

FEBRUARY 28, 1979

Marilyn came into my room and I asked her, "Who is the president?" Then I turned to mom, "Thank you for all the times you visit me."

Mom said, "You're welcome. Pam, how come you asked dad, why we didn't have more children?"

"Because, if I had died, Marilyn would be alone."

MARCH 1979.

With each new day, came another improvement to my body. I spoke constantly, with whomever would listen. As the weeks went by, I progressed at a rapid pace.

It's raining today and I am in speech class. Diane, the speech therapist began, "OK, who can tell me today's date?" I raised my hand. "Pam" "It's March 1, 1979."

Life at Rancho, was like entering into a different dimension. You were surrounded with heartbreaking tragedies of different sorts. Living with people who, by no choice of their own, had been challenged with facing the hardship of losing their independence and having to learn how to fit in once again.

These patients are dealing with not only the horror of what has happened to them, they are having to deal with the depression that surrounds it.

I couldn't even visualize the years ahead at that point of my recovery. What I wasn't prepared for, even though being warned, was that the anger I held onto would be buried deep down inside of me. I was one angry woman. It just was not fair what happened to me. I wanted to be normal again. People just ruthlessly stare at someone with a handicap. Sometimes it's just plain curiosity, other times it's a freak show and there was no way I wanted to be a part of one. I was one bitter individual.

*   *   *

PAM AND HEAD NURSE DOROTHY

It's now late March and the alarm clock is ringing beside mom's bed. She rolls over and no Jimmy. Goes out into the hall and calls his name, "Jimmy."
A faint answer,

"I'm in the kitchen, Rosie." She walks through the hall, yawning. Then says, "Morning honey, Pam keeps asking where you are. Feel like making a trip down to Rancho with me?"

He looks up from his paper, "I have to meet with some clients later."

"What's more important Jim? Visiting with your daughter and showing her that she's worth your time, or some client that may or may not pan out?"

Tears began streaming from his eyes, "I don't know how you do it. Seeing her day in and day out like that. I feel so cheated by what has happened and then to be faced with it constantly. I just can't do it." Mom just squeezed his arm and said,

"Jim, if you saw the day to day improvements, you'd know. She's coming back to us, it's going to happen."

My dad Jim, wasn't the type who could see past the present, and did not want to accept what had been taken away. His little Pammy was going to be someone and now look.

* * *

My tracheotomy has been removed and replaced by a wide bandage across my throat. Ever since then my hangout was the hallway ashtray, much to my dad's disgust. But, for me it was a sign of independence. I could actually do something that I decided to do, smoke a cigarette. What an accomplishment.

I had been wheeling by the ashtray day after day, where my friend Tom hung out. One day I stopped and decided to join him, "Hey Tom, got a smoke?"

He smiles, digs one out of his pack and holds up a lighter.

"Thanks." I say, exhaling in his face.

It had been a few months, so the first drag actually made me dizzy. He backed up his chair on the other side of the ashtray and lit one for himself. That was the beginning of my days at the ashtray. In time, we acquired a titled known as, The Hall Hoodlums.

Tom was such a dear. He was one of the head injured patients on Ward 804, the Head Trauma ward. Yes, so was I. Neither of us had any Cognitive level damage, in other words, we communicated just fine. Although, I cannot remember what had happened to Tom to put him here, he had similar injuries to me.

I do remember that, recently before his injury, his girlfriend and he had a baby. I also remember hearing, that his girlfriend broke up with him after his accident. Tom turns to me, takes a swallow and forms the words,

"When are you gettin out of here?"

"Can't be soon enough," I said, "I think they're talking

about putting me on parole for the weekends." I look at my watch, "Whoops, I'm gonna be late for therapy."
I push the cigarette in the ashtray and start to wheel away.

My right hand reaches for the wheel with my left arm curled in my lap, left foot on the rest, while the right foot is struggling to keep me forward. The hallway is filled with patients in their wheelchairs, parked along the sides. I am slowly maneuvering my chair, push then stop, as it begins to turn crooked.

Oh yuck, there's Gus the gang member and he's right in my pathway. Should I be scared? No way, this is my hallway too. I'm inching by, my left hand laying on my tummy, left foot on the footrest, right hand and foot doing their best to get me there, without going in circles.

Push then stop, push then stop, when I notice him starting to squint his eyes and growl at me. Well, that was all that it took to make me furious in those days, so I backed my chair up beside his and began to kick the spokes of his wheel, while screaming, "You jerk!" *With each kick, I gave him a reason. I'd say,* "... and this one is for laughing at me when I was on that Tilt Table!" *Then I spit at him. I looked back at Tom who was laughing.* He had no problems with Gus.

Each patient had their own things to deal with and so didn't really involve themselves with one another's difficulties.

That part was up to the therapists.

Sandy ran out, grabbed for the handles on my chair and rushed me away. Back at the gym, she grabbed my arm and said,

"Now what was that all about?"

"I don't know," I smirked. "I just needed to scream at that idiot."

Sandy squeezed me tighter and said, "But the time has come for you to understand something. You have been so fortunate Pam, and most patients on this ward are not as lucky. They cannot even communicate, but they need the same love and compassion that you were given. Now do you understand?"

"OK, I'm sorry, if I am still gonna get paroled. Am I?" That was all I could think about. Sandy chuckles,

"Of course Pam, now let's get some work done."

The next six months were like growing up all over again. Only this time, you had to learn by your mistakes, if you wanted to get better. This hospital is considered to be the most proficient institution in the West, but as a patient, it was hard to comply, knowing just how much it would require of you.

* * *

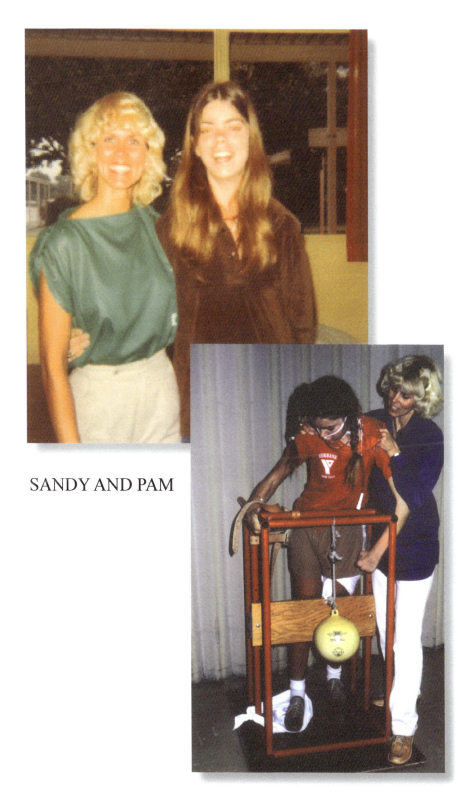

SANDY AND PAM

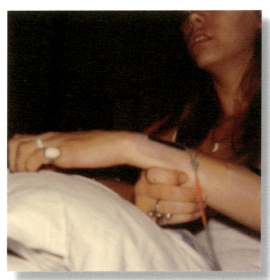

ELECTRODE PATCHES ON MY ARM
The electrodes were used to stimulate my muscles.

DR.GARLAND, PAM AND SANDY

Monday morning.

Time for rounds again. I am sitting on my bed when Doctor Garland and a group of medical students, interns and residents as well as the allied health professionals, enter.

"Hi Pam," Dr. Garland greeted me with a smile.

"Hi Gar," I responded.

He smiled again and began reading from his notes, since he was the chief.

"This patient is Pamela Jansen. She was in an automobile accident and sustained a traumatic head injury.

"Pam," Dr. Garland held his hands towards me, to assist me in standing. "I want you to walk for us using your cane."

I stood up, with the help of doctor, and then began to walk.

"Now, take note of how her Left foot is turning inward and downward. It is inverting, causing her to sway," Dr. Garland continued,

"A splatt, split of the anterior tibial tendon transfer, is necessary to transfer part of the tendon to the outside of the foot to neutralize the force."

Days later, I was wheeled into the preop room and parked beside a girl who I'd met earlier. Sally was sitting up on her gurney, looking around.

Oh boy, someone to talk to. I said to myself in relief. I'd been lying down on my gurney and so I lifted my head and said to her,

"Hi Sally, what are you having done?"

"They're going to cut off my leg", she said so nonchalantly.

"Oh, I'm sorry," I said, trying not to sound shocked. My head dropped back to my pillow, my eyes, likely the size of quarters. The nurse approached to give me a shot of Demerol, which was the initial step to preparing for surgery. I whispered something and she couldn't hear, so she leaned over closer. I whispered,

"They're going to cut off her leg. There's no chance of us being mixed up, is there?"

The nurse smiled and comforted me, "No honey, I'll make sure that they don't." She lifted my arm to point to the ID bracelet on my wrist, "They always look at your name, before starting to operate."

As the shot began to take effect, I laid there, blinking my eyes constantly, so that I'd stay awake until I was in the operating room. I knew that once I saw Dr. Gar's face, I'd be assured that I was safe.

I was so frightened that Sally and I were going to be mistaken for each other and that I'd wake up with one leg.

"Hey Pam", Gar greeted me, as the anesthesiologist was holding the mask for my face.

"Hi Doc, OK good night," I remarked just before the mask was placed, over my mouth and nose. One, two, three, fou..., I'm in dreamland.

This surgery was to perform the SPLATT. The major advantage would be that my foot would no longer twist with the outside of my foot on the floor.

This would prevent wearing a brace or causing me to twist my ankle without it. I awoke hours later, with both legs. My left foot had a cast, that came to just below my knee.

*   *   *

Then there came the recuperation. Physical therapy taught me how to walk again, strengthening the muscles and retraining reflex action. Occupational therapy trained me to use my hands with coordination again. Speech therapy trained me to once again enunciate, enhancing communication with the outside world.

Finally, there was counseling therapy, to try and prepare me for just that, the outside world. If I had known then what I was about to face, I don't know if I would have made it this far. I just could not see myself injured as severely as the people around me.

Sure there were complications, but they were going to heal in no time. Isn't that a taste of the mercy of God? He reveals to us only what we are able to handle at that moment. God was bringing me through a major process. There was so much to learn about God throughout this journey, in His time.

*   *   *

Late APRIL 1979. The sun is rising, and I'm lying in bed in my hospital room, trying to wake up and face another day. The meal cart, which was my alarm clock in a place like Rancho Los Amigos, is rolling down the hall, with the aromas of coffee, oatmeal and bacon.

It's Friday, parole day. I get to face the outside world again, after being confined to these hospital grounds for what seemed to be an eternity, when actually, it's only been about three and a half months. Also, it has been with people who are either used to seeing disabilities or with people who have one themselves. Am I going to like this? To finally compare myself with the outside world? I don't know.

Another sign of my independence has been added to my list of accomplishments. My wheelchair is parked beside my bed, so I have the freedom to roam the halls whenever I want.

My body is a bit stiff today, my muscles weak. I wonder when I'm gonna be able to stand and walk to my wheel chair. Up to that point, the only way to get out of bed, was to have my wheel chair parked beside me. I had not as of yet, been able to use my cane, without having someone by my side, to hold my left arm.

Those all too familiar scenes from my past begin flashing by. There I am at 16 years old, auditioning for Ice Capades at the Los Angeles Forum.

What a tough predicament, being so disabled but with a clear memory of how I was able to do things with little effort.

Scenes kept flashing by. I was ice skating at the Los Angeles Forum.

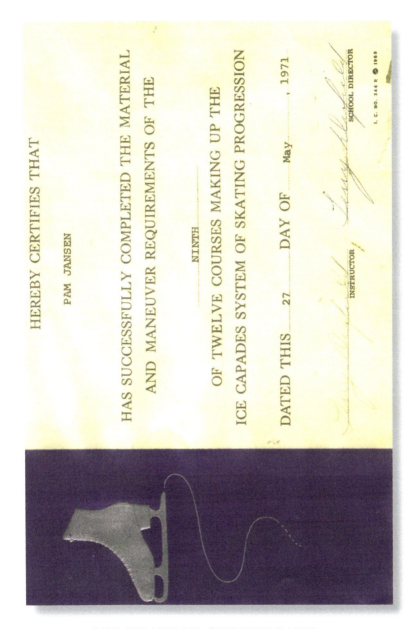

HEREBY CERTIFIES THAT

PAM JANSEN

HAS SUCCESSFULLY COMPLETED THE MATERIAL
AND MANEUVER REQUIREMENTS OF THE

NINTH

OF TWELVE COURSES MAKING UP THE
ICE CAPADES SYSTEM OF SKATING PROGRESSION

DATED THIS _____ 27 _____ DAY OF ___ May ___ , 1971

INSTRUCTOR

SCHOOL DIRECTOR

I. C. NO. 344 R © 1969

ICE SKATING CERTIFICATE

Mom walks into my room and I am brought back to reality.

"Hi Pam, today's the day! I need to check with the staff about taking your medication." She begins to gather my things, by grabbing my suitcase and tossing clothes in.

"Hi mom."

This is an exciting day, but for the moment, all I am thinking about is a cup of coffee. Heading down the hall to breakfast, my right side is doing all of the work to get me there. Left arm still curled over my tummy, left foot on the footrest. Traveling at a rate of, push then stop, push then stop, push then stop. *Damn, what a drag. I don't want to be like this any longer! It is no fun!* Push then stop.

Oh no, Gus that gang member is near the door. Now that I know his name, maybe he won't be so mean to me. I wonder if Gus even remembers. I can't believe that I bent the spokes on his wheelchair. The closer I come, the damage that I did with every kick to his wheel shows up.

I am becoming more and more nervous as I approach him. *Oh God, I hope he doesn't recognize the side of my head.* I am holding my breath, as I pass him, push then stop, push then stop. He didn't even remember me though. *Hallelujah, I don't want to risk having my parole taken away.*

The breakfast room was set up for around twenty five patients, and since I didn't speed down, there is only one empty space with a tray left.

Most of us cannot even walk, so the trays were placed side by side on the tables. I am trying to be so quiet, so that Gus, the gang member, doesn't notice me and maybe spark a memory.

The empty space was right next to my buds, Tom and Marty, and even though it was not between them, I wheeled up and squeezed my chair in, keeping my head low. Tom looks at me and smiles because he knew what I was doing, by trying to be discreet.

He had witnessed the results of the encounter and the damage I did to Gus's spokes and thought that it was too funny. Marty, on the other hand, had such a mild temperament, that was helpful for me to be exposed to.

MARTY AND PAM BAKING A CAKE. ME? SMILE?

59

Tom was the naughty side of me. He was my Hall Hoodlum partner when smoking cigarettes. We'd sit at that ashtray and laugh as we cussed out the way we felt about life now. I had to have that smart alec side in order to endure my situation. Fortunately my memory was intact, but it was sad to remember what I was like then. I was athletic, strong and could walk fast without help.

Marty was like an angelic side. He was just so mild mannered. I think that I offended him when I'd spurt out bad words, because he'd just look down.

A Hispanic attendant came by to pour my coffee. Hank was so sweet. He had the greatest sense of humor. I am sure that was a requirement to be around us, daily. Hank was a natural though. You could tell that he loved his job, as he strutted his stuff alongside the tables.

"Morning Pam, coffee?"

"Love it Hank. Can I have a straw?" I asked him.

"You sure can."

He pulled one out of his other hand.

I still couldn't tip a cup safely and my good side was suffering with ataxia. Ataxia is defined as an inability to coordinate muscular movement. I shook when I tried to drink and sometimes when I didn't use a straw, my coffee splashed to the floor.

"Hi Pam," Tom said, while not looking especially joyful, and my grin was most likely from ear to ear. "what's new?" Should I tell him my news? Marty looks at me with those captivating eyes,

"Pam, I hear that you're getting away."

Thanks Marty, I thought to myself.

"I have to be back tonight guys. It's not that big of a deal." I reached for my spoon and finished as fast as I could. With my final swallow, I unlock my wheels and push out from the table,

"Bye, guys." *I wheeled away, push then stop, push then stop, but this time, I found myself looking side to side, no Gus.*

*   *   *

Back at my room, mom piles a suitcase on my lap, stuffs my bag of medication beside my leg.

"Comfortable?" mom asked.

"I sure am. Now let's get the hell out of this San Quentin."

Mom grabbed the handles of my chair and we began the long awaited departure. We get to the curb, in the parking lot, mom locks my wheels, and goes to get the car. The routine of what will be for years to come is now forming, as mom pulls up, gets out to help me into the car, puts my wheelchair in the trunk, and returns.

It has been so long since I've been on a freeway that I don't even remember the last time. The sky is a little smoggy, but it is so exciting to be, "On The Road Again."

Willie Nelson has become the narrator of my recovery. Starting with, my wheelchair days, and inching down the hall, "Don't Get Around Much Anymore" and Marty's, "Blue Eyes Cryin In The Rain".

I had such anticipation of good things about to happen.

"Pam, why don't we stop at the studios?"

I look at her hesitantly, "I'm scared to let my friends see me now mom, I walk and talk like I'm drunk."

"Pam, you just said it, they're friends."

"But mom I'm so embarrassed, I don't want them to see me like this."

She reached across the seat for my hand, while driving, "You don't need to be scared, because if they're your friends, they'll love you no matter what."

We pulled up and parked in the lot across from Burbank Studios, and the routine takes place, with mom getting out and heading for my chair in the trunk.

I am in, what has been recently labeled, The Blue Mercedes, my wheelchair, and so we head to the gate. The guard remembers me and so waves us through, to my unveiling.

"Where should I go Pam?" mom said with an anxious tone. I guess that she was nervous too. I am just so hesitant to show my mangled body, even though I wanted to see those guys badly. I really missed them.

"Turn right, past this first row of buildings."

The sounds of hammers pounding and saws buzzing were a welcome home for me.

Passing a stage on our way, some faces turn towards me in shock, "Pam", someone yelled and a group of guys hurried over. There I was, in a wheelchair no less, and they were glad to see me. I felt so self conscious and each one of them leaned over to hug me. They were actually happy to see me, even if it was in this condition.

The crowd of friends increased, giving hugs, while a foreman is standing in the background frowning, his arms folded, looking at his watch, and tapping his foot impatiently. Supposedly, his way of signaling the guys, to get back to work. There isn't a moment of hesitation, as everyone said their goodbyes and went back.

We decided not to go any further, after experiencing that look from the foreman and knowing that we were interrupting a work day. After the routine has been taken care of, pulling up to the car, parking the chair, putting me in, placing the chair in the trunk, we started towards home and I began to feel so sad. I missed my life as it was.

Mom could sense what I was feeling, especially after having a taste of what it was like to be around such an atmosphere. We didn't bump into any movie stars that day, but it was the energy of the surroundings at the studios.

Because of everything that happened to me, I was such an angry woman, and it did not end for years. There it is, home. We pull up to the curb and park. Mom was doing everything to make sure that, she was acting according to protocol.

"Now Pam, let me walk you up the driveway."

"Mom, please don't do this to me. I want to be normal again."

She loved me so much that anyone would find it difficult to witness the challenges she is about to have thrown in her face.

"I know honey, but this is new for both of us. Have patience, OK?"

With squinted eyes and my teeth gritted, I began to push my body off the seat, out of the car, with my cane in my left hand. That faithful right hand pushed as hard as it could. I am up and dad rushes out, "Hi Bosco," He grabbed me in his arms. It's as if you are visiting a place that you know belongs to you, but you're on a pass, you can't stay.

Memories of past freedoms are coming back, and frustration was building. We are sitting down at dinner, and I blurt out,

"I'm going out for awhile after dinner with some friends."
I didn't know who, but I was going to try. Mom aggressively responds,

"You can't. I need to take you back to the hospital by 9:00."

At that response, I pick up my tostada and heave it at the wall. Refried beans are dripping down, while tears stream down my cheeks,

"Stop telling me what to do! I'm 21 years old,"
I screamed out.

I was just beginning to understand what had been taken away and it wasn't pretty. Dad put his head in his hands, and whispered, "I don't know about this." I just grabbed for the lock release of my wheels, with my right hand reaching across to my left wheel. Frustration overflowed, as I backed up and headed for my old bedroom.

Scraping the door frame, because the house was not set up for wheelchairs and slammed the door behind me. I reached the bed, locked the wheels on my chair, and rolled into it. I was distraught laying there, thinking about my life and what it had become. Memories...

Man, we need to be prepared to handle anything that is dished out.

After a while, there's a knock on the door.

"Who is it?" I angrily respond.

"It's mom, honey. If we want to get back on time, we need to start getting ready to leave. Remember Pam, this is parole, to see how you manage in the outside world. If we don't cooperate the first time, we'll lose the privilege."

I don't even respond. I just slide my butt onto the wheelchair, and head for the bathroom, when once again, my wheels scrape the molding. Dad is walking by and I turned around to see the back of his head turning from side to side.

"I can't help it!" I screamed.

Mom comes to help me to the car. "Now Pam," she said, "Let me walk you down the driveway to the car. Dad can put the chair in the trunk." "Whatever," I respond.

On the freeway, heading back, I screamed, "Mom, why did this happen to me? I don't want to go back to that prison. Why are you forcing me?"

Teardrops are running down mom's face as she drives.

"Pam, this is the most qualified hospital around, for your kind of injury. They're helping you."
Still screaming, I answer, "But mom, I don't want to go back, it's my life!"
Mom doesn't even want to carry on, so she keeps silent. She knew that it would just feed fuel to the argument.

Quieted down after an exhausting tantrum,
we reach the hospital grounds.

"San Quentin," I sarcastically state. I was beginning to learn that the exhaustion was just not worth it. We park and the routine takes place, as mom pushed me up to the nurses' counter and signed me in at 8:50 pm.

"Here we are, we made it back with minutes to spare." Mom said. I blankly stare into space,

"Good job mom, I'm sure the warden will be pleased."

Not in the mood to greet anyone, I quietly
ask, while staring into space,

"Now, would you push me to my bed?"

APRIL 23, 1979.

I am 22 years old today. What a life, now. I can't even walk alone. People have trouble understanding me when I talk, I am no longer driving. My freedom has been taken away. My life is under constant surveillance. I'm in this prison of a hospital.

Elsie, my other physical therapist, walks into my room and says to me,

"Good morning Pam, I hear it's your birthday today. Well, Happy Birthday and you can receive this as a present. We've decided to remove the tilt table from your regimen."

"Oh my God," I was ecstatic, "you're playing with me. No more torture?"

"Nope."

*   *   *

The days are passing at an even pace now. Months ago, it seemed as if years would pass before I would be set free. Now that my mind is more alert, I can see that Rancho Los Amigos is really beneficial. I worked daily with a certified therapist and my progress was monitored, noting any difficulties that were slowing down my healing.

They were then conveyed to Doctor Garland the Chief Orthopedic Surgeon. When surgical procedure would prove to be advantageous, it would take place.

MAY 1979.

Throughout the weeks, this old body is improving at a rapid pace. I am now walking around, but I still need someone at my side. One day, Sandy approaches me to ask something.

"Pam, want to hear some good news? The staff got together to discuss your progress, and decided that you have reached the goal. You're being released this Monday! It's time to take control, as if you haven't already. Isn't that exciting?"

I don't know how to respond, but I look back in astonishment,

"Really?" *I picture those awful elephant heads. I won, ha!*

"Pam," Sandy continues, "the rest of the staff strongly encourages a meeting with Sarah. You and your mom should sit down with her before your discharge. You both are going to need to be aware of what you are about to face."

"Are you trying to make me aware of how different I am now? My friends are going to love me no matter what." *I didn't know then how much denial I was in.*

*   *   *

.

68

JUNE 1979.

It's Monday morning, when mom and I are sitting in Sarah's office. I am staring out the window, while she talks with mom. Sarah began by saying,

"Pam is finally going home today. After six months with us, she's become accustomed to the protective environment, so she'll have to learn to deal with the outside world once again. Only this time, it's with a handicap. It won't be easy because she's bright and wants her life back."

Mom nods, "I know she's going to need our support now, more than ever."

Sarah continues, "This is true Rosie. She's going to suffer tremendous frustration. In one sense, she's going to have to grow up all over again. Remember in the beginning, when she awoke, it took her weeks just to eat some baby food?"

Mom listens intently, as Sarah goes on, "She'll have to learn to fit in with the crowds she was once so comfortable with. Pam's a different person now, and the sooner she accepts it, the sooner emotional healing will begin. She won't realize it right away, but it can be thrown in her face when she least expects it and that's where you'll come in. Survival may seem impossible then Rosie, but it isn't. Don't give up."

Even though I appeared to be inattentive, everything Sarah expressed, registered. After all, this meeting was for both of us. It was to try and make me aware of how to handle what I was about to face and boy was I in for an awakening. Here it is, for once to be able to call the shots, after six and a half months. What I wasn't prepared for, was my life in others' eyes now. I would no longer be regarded as an independent woman.

The onset of the loneliest years of my life had begun. None of my friends could handle being around me for more than an hour. Why, I wondered. I didn't smell or anything like that. I guess it was because I was unable to carry on a conversation without them straining to understand my words, or maybe that I was a reminder of what could so easily happen to them. I don't know.

One of my good friends told me that it was a hassle taking me to parties now. In essence, this 22 year old would be growing up all over again, with the need to prove that I was capable. I had to be whole again.

Our meeting with Sarah came to an end and it was time to say goodbye. I felt somewhat sad, leaving the people I began my day with for the past six months. Marty had already returned to Michigan. Tom was there to say goodbye though.

"Hang on Pam, we're heading out, for the last time."

"OK, but remember my goal mom? I set it back in February or March, I don't remember, but I looked at you and said, "I am going to walk out of those doors."

"Are you sure, Pam? OK, let me lock the wheels on your chair and help you stand."

"Mom, while I'm holding on to you for dear life, will you hand me my cane?"

"I will, don't worry, you won't fall" I'm beginning to push off of the chair handle and suddenly my hand latches onto mom's bent forearm.

"You're safe honey, now grab onto the cane."

"This is so cool, mom. Thank you."

We approach those huge metal doors, mom holding my left arm, my right hand gripping the handle of the cane.

"Yeah Pam," everyone who was watching yelled out from down the hall.

"Here we are. You made it in twenty minutes."

"Yeah, a two minute walk mom," I'm just rolling my eyes. Mom opens the door for me and we're off, waving goodbye to a part of my life that was just the beginning to a road back.

*　　*　　*

SECTION FOUR

LATE JUNE 1979.

We're at Saint Joseph Hospital in Burbank, California, and mom is signing me up for Outpatient Therapy. She comes back to sit on the couch beside my wheelchair. I am crying and I look to her,

"Mom, I feel like I'll always be like this, and no one's ever gonna love me. I'm scared that I'll never be needed again." She hugs me, fighting back her own tears.

The receptionist, Marguerite came in the room and said,

"OK Pam, they're ready now." She was pretty cheerful, and that was a nice welcome. She takes control of my chair and pushes me into the gym. Mom stayed in the waiting room, watching TV.

At the gym, I am sitting there in my chair, not knowing what to expect. People were being so friendly. This was not the same atmosphere as Rancho Los Amigos, because you weren't surrounded with tragedy. Since this wasn't a head injury ward, I felt a bit more at ease. No Gus, the gang member, to hide from either.

A very warm and friendly therapist walks up to me and says, "Hi Pam, I'm Holly and we'll be working together."

"Hi Holly," *I was so thankful for the respect I had received.*

"First I want to get you on the mat to see how you do with range of motion."

Holly was so nice to me. I realized that since this wasn't a Head Injury Ward, I'd come from an atmosphere where I had accepted being less of a person than most. I am, incredibly thankful though, to have begun recuperation at Rancho Los Amigos Hospital, because that hospital held so much expertise.

The surroundings in the gym at Saint Joseph's were similar, except there was no tilt table. Hallelujah.

Holly wheeled me up to the mat, locked my wheels, and helped me stand up, turn my butt toward the mat, and sit.

"Good one Pam, now I want you to lay back, so I can stretch you."

Uh oh, stretch me, ouch. I leaned to my right, then shifted over on my back. Oh boy, here it comes.

"I want to see how loose you are."

First, Holly lifted my right arm, which after six months, had become relaxed enough. Then the left one, which was still so tight. Holly said,

"I'm sorry Pam, I need to do this to record your progress from the start."

Then came the legs. Same thing as Holly tested the right, then the left.

"Oh, sorry Pam, just a bit more."

I am gritting my teeth. The pain is like I am being forced to do the splits. She placed my leg back on the mat and wrote some notes. This first visit was an evaluation to know what level I was at.

On our way home, I look at mom, "I'm gonna get better and better, huh?"

"That is why you were so fortunate to spend so long at Rancho Los Amigos, Pam. They helped you start and now Saint Joseph's is going to polish everything."

As I said, I had damaged the part of my brain, the Cerebellum which fine tunes, speech, balance and motor control. In the years to come, I would have numerous surgeries to fix what had gone wrong. Over time, my voice improved, but it would never again return to its original state.

My father became less and less patient with the antics I performed, due to my own lack of patience. One day we were talking about my life and how it has dramatically changed, when I added to the conversation by saying, "My happy ending is going to be to meet someone and fall in love with life all over again."

"No one's ever going to love you. You're handicapped!" he yelled, while pointing his finger in my face. I looked him in the eyes, then leaned over and spit on the carpeting. He was so mad that he grabbed my arm and pulled me out of my wheelchair, where I landed on the floor, spitting in my face.

"Leave me alone!" I screamed. "You're just damn lucky mom's at work. You know that she'd stick up for me!" He just shook his head and walked away.
I used my right hand and leg to climb back into my wheelchair.

My dad loved me so much but in his own way. He didn't know how to show it aside from the frustration of what his little girl, Pammy had become.

*   *   *

1980

My parents house, where I'd been living, since I was released from Rancho Los Amigos, wasn't the ideal location for my recovery. I was literally housebound. The house was situated on a small hill, so I wasn't able to wheel outside by myself.

Marilyn was also living there. Four adults, two bedroom house with one bathroom. One afternoon, I'm sitting at my parents house, bored to death, when Marilyn drives up.

She ran up to the house, opened the door, approached me and excitedly began,

"Pam, we're going to make a change. You need more people around you! You and I are going to enroll at Valley College. Not only that, I found an apartment right across the street!"

I was so ecstatic that tears filled my eyes. "Things are going to change, for the better, aren't they? Oh my God, thank you Marilyn," I gleefully expressed.

"OK Pam, now registration is this evening, or we can go tomorrow morning."

"Tonight's the night!" I screamed.

"OK," Marilyn answered, while planning our steps on a piece of paper, "we can even look at the apartment." She reached for my cane, locked my wheels and helped me stand up.

"Now, go change clothes. If you need any help, I'll be right here."

"Oh my God, I am there." I said, while walking away, step then stop, step then stop. Right then, mom's car pulled up. "Let me handle this Pam," Marilyn said. Mom walked in, "Hi, where's Pam?"

"Hi mom, how was your day?" Marilyn began and before mom could even answer, she said, "Pam is changing clothes to go and register for school." Mom was a bit stunned, "What school? Where?"

"Mom," Marilyn began, "if Pam keeps up this routine of just going to therapy and coming home, she'll never regain her life. She needs outside stimulation. She needs to be exposed to other avenues of influence that will build her motivation to live a full life."

"But my baby..." mom started.

"Mom, she's not a baby, she's 23 years old!" Marilyn interrupted.

"You're right Marilyn," she said.

"Oh mom," Marilyn continued, "I've also found us an apartment across the street from Valley College. We'll be checking it out tonight." Mom just began to cry. Right then, I walked into the room, step then stop, step then stop. I looked at her, sitting there, "Hi mom, you OK?"

"Just go do what you need to do," she sobbed. I just kept silent, because inside, I was so excited.

"Hey Pam, I'll walk you down to the car," Marilyn said, while placing my wheelchair near the door, "but we'll need this chair because it is a long walk."

"Do I really need the wheelchair?"

"Pam, come on, it will takes us twice as long without it."

At that point of my life, I was still resentful, because of the things that I wasn't able to do.

*　*　*

We arrived at the college parking lot and I raised my eyebrows and asked, "Think that you could just push me to the door, and we'll leave the chair outside of the auditorium, Mare?"

Marilyn responded, "OK, but why?"

I looked at her, "I hate this thing."

"Whatever you want Pam, but you won't be the only student in a chair," she said, trying to appear as if she understood.

She then got my chair, the Blue Mercedes out of the trunk and came around to my door.

"We're just going in to choose classes, register and go across the street to look at the apartment, OK? Pam, what do you think about taking a ceramics class to keep your hands moving?" Marilyn asked.

"Ceramics, I took that back in high school. How fun, I'll try it again." I excitedly answered.

"OK, let's go for it," she said trying to pick up the pace. We approached the building and I noticed a few other wheelchairs.

"OK, I'll stay in the chair, Mare." *I had decided, realizing that I wasn't going to stand out.*

"Thanks Pam, what changed your mind?"

"I feel like I can belong, even with this awful disability," I expressed.

"Pam, what happened to you was definitely awful, but you don't look awful."
We went in and got the necessary forms.

"Look at this Pam," Marilyn said, while fanning through a pamphlet, "We should sign up for a Photography class." That's just what we did, so a Ceramics class and a photography class were what we ended up with.

*   *   *

"OK, now the apartment," Marilyn was checking her list. When we got to the apartment, it was on the second story with a front and back door.

"This is gonna be great exercise for me, at the same time." I was just so excited to have a place of our own, but close enough to mom and dad's.

We rented it that night and moved in, within a week of starting school.

At this point in my recovery, I wanted my independence back, no matter what! One morning, I awoke and quietly got ready for school, so I could go by myself, without the hideous cane, that I'd become so dependent on.

I snuck down the stairs and walked to the curb, no cane. After a few steps, I needed to lean on a tree for balance. Wouldn't you know it? Of course, being a Junior College, a Narcotics Officer pulls over.

"Hello Miss, where are you headed," he said in an uncertain manner, trying to figure me out. It was too funny, for me not to find humor in this. I laughed, "I live right up there. I'm handicapped and I want to start walking without my cane, so I left home without it. I'm just taking a rest." I told him my name and shook his hand.

"OK Pam, just be careful." He was smiling as he said, "Goodbye."

"Pam," Marilyn yelled from the apartment window, "what are you doing, out there alone?"

"I'm going to school!" I yelled back.

"Wait for me! I'll grab our stuff for photography."

"Hurry, so we can get a darkroom."

We had film to develop. At school, we entered one of the developing rooms.

"This is such good therapy for me, to stand in the pitch black, open a film canister and wind the film strip onto a reel, then add the chemicals."

We stayed in that apartment for about a year, and then I temporarily moved back to mom and dad's place.

*   *   *

JULY 1982.

Mom and I are having our morning coffee and I am just sitting at the table, planning my life.

"Mom, I want to start driving again."
She looked back at me and said, "Pam, that's a big step. Wow, I'll need to check with your Doctor, first.

The first day of my drivers training, was an evaluation allowing them to test my reaction levels. First the parking lot, then the streets.

I got into the car, wondering if maybe some memories of the accident would return and I'd freak out. Actually, it was like sitting down, looking forward and saying, long time no see. It just felt so natural to me that, throughout the weeks, everything went smooth as could be.

"OK Pam," Sam said while signing a clipboard, "you've successfully completed the program. We're done, now drive us back."

"Hey Sam," I turned to him, "OK if I drive through a Jack In The Box? I want to practice driving through and ordering, then to see how I do reaching for the food after I pay."

81

"OK Pam," Sam continued, "but you're going to need to pay."

"Of course, I will. Would you like anything?"
I pulled in, ordered, and on the way up to the window, I went up the curb. My instructor covered his eyes and laughed. I could still laugh at myself.

In August of 1982, my driver's license was renewed! I was so happy that I could go somewhere, by myself.

One morning, I pulled into the parking lot of the May Company department store. I got out and took the elevator down. The doors opened at the basement and I began to step out, passing this older woman.

All of a sudden, the woman snickered. I looked at her, with her hand over her mouth, when she began to say, "Scuse me, but I broke my hip awhile ago," she couldn't stop chuckling, "and thank God I don't look that bad!"

I just froze and stared in disbelief and not wanting to say something bad, I turned and walked away. I managed to get a few steps away, when I stopped, turned back and said, "That was a terrible thing to say. I was so frustrated at myself, I stood there thinking, *why can't I have things back to normal all at once, damn. Things had better look up, or else,* I thought.

I drove home, walked in the house, step than stop. *I have got to make a change.* I began to check out rentals, in the newspaper and found a perfectly, darling guest house in Burbank, California and moved in that week. The guesthouse fit my needs perfectly, for that time in my life.

I had a routine for my daily activities, which, day by day held more and more meaning. It started off simple, when Beth, a therapist back at Rancho Los Amigos had noticed my left side sag as I walked. She devised a way for me to break the pattern.

My assignment for the time being was to push a shopping cart, and in so doing, my body was standing straight up. I went to Ralphs Grocery every day and pushed a cart around the store. The manager said that it would be OK so, I'd do about twenty laps. I felt as if I was showing up for work and should fill out a time card.

I'd buy groceries such as, chicken, fresh vegetables, potatoes, juice and snacks, always a yogurt and of course animal crackers to dip in it while doing my laps. My sister Marilyn would come over and look in my freezer at zip lock bags, each with a single serving. That way, if someone wanted to have dinner over, I'd just pull another bag out. The thing was, I didn't get to pull extra bags out that often. It was a very lonely time in my life.

*   *   *

One day an old boyfriend, knowing what I had been through, invited me to a Bible study. At the study they mentioned going to church in Westwood known as the Hiding Place, and would I like to go?

I thought heck, I've tried everything else so, "OK, let's go."

The following Sunday, we walked into a crowded church, which was actually a high school auditorium. There were very different kinds of people, but you could sense by the calm spirits that everyone appeared to be in the right place. It was an existence of just so much love and acceptance.

We found some seats and while I was listening to the sermon, I looked over at my friends and thought, OK who told the pastor about me. I didn't know it then, but the Holy Spirit had me hook, line, and sinker.

That was a day of relief for me, because I felt so much peace. I gained new hope that my life was going to change for the better.

After a year of attending the Church, I met someone, a fellow Christian that was interested in getting to know me. He had just joined. As we became more involved, he ended up taking me to healing seminar after seminar. When the speaker gave an invitation for people who needed prayer for a miracle, I went up, just begging the Lord to heal me.

Finally, one night after a Bible study, Danny and I were sitting in his car. He was looking straight ahead and said,

"I don't know if I can handle this, I mean, I'm a proud person."

He was talking about being seen with me, I knew.

"But Danny, I'm getting so much better."

He wanted someone now and she had to look good. Oh well. I just got out of his car and into my own. No way, I was going to react wrong because he'd probably tell the Pastor.

I've learned over the years that once you accept Christ in your heart, it's not always an immediate change. It took me twenty years to arrive at this level of understanding and I am still arriving. I've heard it compared to the peeling of an onion, it happens layer by layer. You know, I'm kind of relieved that it's happened that way, because now I can look back and learn from my mistakes, realizing that Jesus is the One who walked on water, not me.

*   *   *

SEPTEMBER 1982.

I decided that it was time to start fine tuning the abilities that were slowly but surely, returning. I just had to be a normal working person again and no matter what it took, my goal was to fit in and not stand out.

I registered at Glendale Community College. Comprehension was a major challenge for me, so I enrolled in Speech, titled as such, but actually it was a class for disabled students, allowing us to get together and talk. I always took it one step further though, by treating it as a class to vent, no matter how rude or obnoxious I'd sound. We'd sit around a table and talk and talk. It was Brad, Jean, Dennis, myself, a few other students and our instructor.

Nancy would bring up a situation of dealing with everyday life, and we'd continue. The group was very honest and if I had allowed, it would've really helped me to face and accept myself. Brad would join in and talk about the struggles of being in a wheelchair, but every time he mentioned the words handicap and we, I flew off the handle. He'd say, "We have to realize..."

"What do you mean, we, Brad? I am not going to realize anything! I don't want to settle for being like this! Damn it."

I just would not accept the fact of being handicapped. I was still in denial, holding onto the stubborn belief that I formed when I was back in Rancho, "Sure I had complications, but they were going to heal in no time."

Disability was not a word that I would associate with my person, or even accept the fact that I was one of them. Or so I thought. I didn't want to be like this for the rest of my life! I hated myself. I used to scream and cuss in that class.

Nancy, our instructor, was so patient and loving, although I am sure that it took quite an effort to put up with my verbal temper tantrums. I'd be set off during a normally calm discussion, and with no warning, I'd scream and cuss at whomever had said something that I didn't agree with. I just could not accept my condition. Pam was getting to know herself through others, and I didn't like me.

My evening class was titled, Drawing From the Right Side of Your Brain. That first night of class, still new in the Lord, I sat there at my desk and whispered,

"Lord, I'm not sure how to talk with you yet, let alone ask You for a favor, but these hands are Yours. Please use them. In Jesus' Name, Amen."

We were taught to concentrate on a picture and without looking, move the pencil slowly and draw the picture we were staring at, to let our eyes guide the pencil. Out of a magazine, the picture I chose to draw was that of Santa Claus.

With the opposite hand I'd used to write with since childhood, I learned to draw with my right hand. Because of my injury, I had lost the motor control of my left side. Well, I'd been left handed for twenty one years and getting to know my right side wasn't easy, because with the brain injury, I had sustained a severe case of ataxia on the right. Remember that, ataxia is defined as an inability to coordinate muscular movement. Despite all of that, I earned a B in the class!

PAM'S SANTA DRAWING

* * *

1985

As I allowed my eyes to be opened day by day, confirmation was about to reveal itself. I remember turning to a program on the television. The hostess began describing a young woman, who accepted the Lord, while viewing the show. He appeared to her.

She said that the Vision was so beautiful that she sat down and painted a picture of it. The hostess went on to say that if anyone would like a copy, to send in. I thought that there was a reason for my turning to that program, so I sent in.

A few weeks later, a large manila envelope arrived, and upon opening it, I saw the Vision that came to me in 1979. The only difference was that, in mine His arms were folded. All that I was concentrating on, were His captivating eyes. Those eyes made me feel such peace.

Within a couple months, another confirmation was about to reveal itself. It was a warm day so I turned my fan on. I was about ten feet away watching as the fan began to turn the pages of an open Bible nearby. All of a sudden, with the fan still blowing, the pages stopped turning. I said,

"Lord, are You trying to tell me something?"
Ah, what the heck, I thought while walking over, then reading the page it had opened to. I came to a passage that began, "But rise and stand on your feet, for I have appeared to you for this purpose. To make you a minister and a witness, to both of the things which thou has seen, and of the things which I have yet to reveal to you."
Acts 26:16-18. New King James Version

You know, to some of us, He has to make it so obvious. I rubbed my head thinking, what does all of this mean?

"Lord, I want to learn more and more about You." I had been attending church almost three years and I began wondering about myself and my direction with the Lord. Was I doing what He wanted? I mean, He appeared to me when I was living so far from Him, and His moral precepts.

I heard about L.I.F.E. Bible College and registered for the fall semester in September 1985. This time, it wasn't just pick and choose classes, it was a four year college. Mom and dad lived only half an hour away, so I'd visit often.

*   *   *

1986

We were studying the Demonic realm. I was sitting at my desk, when I opened my book to an illustration that looked so familiar. I remembered where I had seen those same characters, only I referred to them as elephant heads. It was when I was on that tilt table back at Rancho, experiencing severe pain and then in times of achievement, those heads were floating by me laughing and breathing fire. In my book was a picture of Demons. It was those elephant heads.

1987

I learned of an overseas Bible study that would be departing in July. The students participating would tour Israel and then study conversational Hebrew in Jerusalem.

At this point of my recovery, I had no second thoughts when it came to an adventure. There was some concern from others, of my being able to endure the trip.

It turned out to be so fulfilling. In the morning we took a class titled Conversational Hebrew and the afternoons were spent exploring Israel. I walked on the same ground where Jesus was born and raised, visiting the sites where He performed Miracles. I went in the Red Sea, floated in the Dead Sea, went in the Sea of Galilee, the River Jordan and the Pool of Siloam.

I walked the Way of Sorrows, where Jesus carried the cross to Calvary. Finally, I visited the tomb where He was laid and three days later He arose.

HEY, HOW ABOUT A RIDE

COME ON, WE'LL BE LATE FOR HEBREW CLASS.

GRADUATION FROM L.I.F.E. BIBLE COLLEGE

MAY 1989

After graduating from L.I.F.E. I knew that God wasn't through teaching me yet. I still had so much anger buried, but I also knew that my story was something to share with people. Being a victim of a severe accident myself, I knew that others could take heed of my existence, not just accident victims, because practically everyone has done something that they're not too proud of. That, I was proof of the possibility of survival.

SEPTEMBER 1990.

I would still go into the hospital gym at Saint Joseph's and work out from time to time. One day, I asked one of the Occupational Therapists what she thought of my becoming an O.T.? She said, "I think you'd be a great example, in fact we could use one here."

"Really? When can I start?"

"Would you be able to on Monday?"

I closed my eyes and remembered sitting in my wheelchair, waiting to begin my first therapy appointment. I was in the waiting room of that very same hospital, when tears were gushing as I cried out to my mom, "I feel like I'm never gonna be needed by anyone again."

WOW!

*   *   *

95

PAMELA JANSEN
OCCUPATIONAL
THERAPY

SISTERS OF
PROVIDENCE

SAINT JOSEPH
MEDICAL CENTER
*Our Standards Are
Simply Higher*

One day after work I decided to stop by mom and dad's house. I walked in their front door and they were both sitting on the couch in the living room. Only this time it just seemed different.

Dad was staring straight ahead with a solemn like stare on his unshaven face. I walked by, heading to the kitchen,

"Hi guys," I kept walking, "what's new?"

"Dad has cancer," mom quietly remarked, "we just got the results."

That stopped me in my tracks. I didn't know what to say. I just looked at my dad sitting there trying to smile and cover up what he was feeling. Him and I were alike in that we always tried to find the humor and so I sat down beside him and elbowed his side and said,

"Finally, someone else gets to play the patient. Not to worry, you'll have three full time nurses, although I do not do bed pans, so that will be someone else's job."
We laughed.

DECEMBER 1990
Christmas shopping that year, held special meaning. Never would I have thought that it would be our last Christmas with dad.

All of us, mom, dad, Marilyn and I went shopping for each other but this time with each other. I bought dad a knee length, plaid nightgown for his homecoming.

DECEMBER 28
Then came the morning of his surgery. All of us, mom, dad, Marilyn and I, went to the hospital that morning. Dad was prepared for surgery upon arrival.

He wore one of those hospital gowns and when he climbed onto the gurney, a surgical cap was placed on him. "Alright dad, nice hat but I could have lent you one," I kidded him. Then they wheeled him away.

*   *   *

After a few hours, the surgeon came out to talk to us and said,

"He did really well. We got all of the cancer, which was the size of a fist and the normal size of a healthy prostate is equal to that of an almond. There was a complication though.

When we pulled at the cancer, there was a small tear in the rectum, due to scar tissue from the previous biopsies. Rectal contents could leak into the bloodstream, so we'll need to watch him closely for the next twenty fours hours in the intensive care unit."

We saw that he was in a lot of pain, as they rolled him by on the way to the recovery unit. We were advised by the Doctor to go home and rest up to return in the morning.

*   *   *

At 5 am the next morning, mom got a call from my dad's nurse saying,

"Mrs. Jansen, you had better come in. Your husband's blood pressure dropped to 50 over 40."

Mom and I rushed back to the hospital, while my sister Marilyn went to McDonald's to get us some breakfast.

By the time we arrived, my dad was nearly in full arrest. They were filling him with IV fluids and hooking him up to every machine available, it seemed. He had gone into septic shock, caused by bacteria that leaked into the blood stream, causing his blood vessels to dilate.

Eventually all of his organs failed. The kidneys, liver and finally his heart gave up after six weeks of being on medication to keep it pumping.

Little did we know that when we dropped him off for his surgery, that we would never speak to him again.

*   *   *

I continued working as an Occupational Therapist Assistant, until late 1992.
SUMMER 1992
My sister Marilyn had been renting a house in the mountains for around one year. She called me and said,

"Hey Pam, come up and spend some time at my house," she was insisting, "it's a beautiful get away You'll love it."

"But Mare, I have a cast on both of my legs," I hesitantly reminded her. She laughed and said, "That's nothing new. What is this now, surgery number 20? I'll drive down and pick you up, come on."

The town she lived in had quite the atmosphere. Imagine that, less than 100 miles from Los Angeles and you were in the woods. It was a playground for bears, deer, chipmunks, squirrels, bears and coyotes.

"OK, when can I move up here?" I laughed.

"I knew that you'd love it," Marilyn said, "wait until we arrive at my house."

We drove for around ten miles more, until we pulled up under the trees and parked beside her cabin. Marilyn jumped out, to grab our bags and she said, "Wait here Pam, I'll walk you up."

I was sitting back and soaking up the surroundings, "This is gorgeous, Mare."

The Blue Jays were chirping, a couple of squirrels were chomping, it was just so serene.

That night, Marilyn fixed up a Futon with comforters and pillows galore for me to sleep on. I slept like a rock buried in such comfort.

At around 6:00 am, I began to stir. Of course, I had to pee. After I did my business, I stood up and all of a sudden, I passed out, falling to the floor.

"Pam," Marilyn screamed. She ran into the bathroom to find me lying on the floor, exhibiting the signs of a Grand Mal seizure.

"Pam," she screamed again. I wasn't able to respond. She felt my arm and my body was cold, my eyes stared straight ahead, as I laid there on the bathroom floor.

"Look at me Pam."

"I'm OK," I mumbled.

I did not respond consciously until thirty minutes later. "Pam, you and I are going back to the valley and have mom take you to Saint Joseph Emergency," Marilyn said.

We drove home, met mom and went directly to the hospital. Of course, the treatment in ER was to load me with Dylantin, an anti-seizure medication which, I had not taken for years.

I was then placed under the care of a doctor and hence began treatment under him, for years of the most deterring waste of time.

This certain doctor had me on so much medication and whenever I called to complain, the dosage was increased. I was taking 2400mg a day.

Finally I began treatment with the care of Dr. Fawaz Faisal, which was a Godsend. He placed me in the UCLA Telemetry ward, where my head was wrapped in gauze, covering numerous EEG tags that were attached to my skull. I remained there for days, under constant monitor while my medicine was decreased, and never had a seizure.

Days later, Dr. Faisal walked into my room, shaking his head as he said, "Pam, you don't even have a seizure disorder."

I knew it.

*   *   *

1993

As time went by, Marilyn had decided to purchase a home, in the area where she had been living. She had been working as nurse for some time now and so, was financially responsible. One day Mom and I went up to her town to look at listings with her.

The realtor opened the front door of one home and with the three of us standing there, we fell in love with it at first sight. Of course, we walked around the inside for awhile, before I stopped her and said,

"Marilyn, I'll buy this with you."
Finally, we turned to Paul Hollingsworth, our realtor, and said, "We'll take it."

*   *   *

My life's direction was about to change. Living in such a beautiful atmosphere was great, but I began to feel so lonely and I did not have any more goals to work toward.

"Marilyn, look at what I got in the mail today. It's an ad for a writer's conference on Maui. I want to share my story, so I'm going to sharpen my skills. You know, living in this beautiful house, in these gorgeous mountains, is awesome, but I feel like I'm once again, wasting my life," I began crying, "I feel like I've lost my goals, and am just existing. Will you go with me? The hotel where it's located is the Grand Wailea."

"Hawaii? Do you need to ask?" Marilyn laughed and continued, "You know Pam, I am so proud of you, that you haven't lost your will to succeed and you have the enthusiasm to push."

"OK," I said excitedly, "I'll find out everything and we'll make our plans, to be there in August."

* * *

August came and we landed on Maui, took a taxi to the Grand Wailea Hotel, which was like stepping into a realm of beauty to be received as royalty. We were now in such a tropical atmosphere. It was dark, but the air was so warm and soothing.

"Let's go register," Marilyn was so organized, "and then see our room."

"I'd really like to shower," I was in awe of this hotel, "and then check out this place."

"Pam, OK if I see about using a wheelchair for the week that we're here?" Marilyn sounded almost apologetic, "this place is huge and we want to see it all."

"Marilyn, haven't you noticed that I just don't care about hiding my disability anymore? I've been missing out on so much, just because I didn't want to be seen like this. But, this is me, now. If I don't love myself, how can I expect anyone I meet to?"

I remembered telling myself that years ago, but never really taking heed to it. We got out of the taxi, walked towards the hotel, and there were greeters standing there with a beautiful flower lei to place on us as they said, "Aloha".

The scents of plumeria and tuberose flowers surrounded the area.

"Hey look Mare," I noticed, "they have a wheelchair waiting."

I stepped over towards the chair, being held by a handsome Hawaiian guy in all white.

"Hi, I mean, Aloha"
He bowed his head and smiled, "Aloha".

"We need to check in and then will you take me to our room?"

"Certainly ma'am."

We got to our room that night and just, passed out, until morning. I awoke to a bird chirping outside my window.

"Morning Mare," I excitedly yelled, "what do you want for breakfast? I'm calling room service."

I'd been saving for this trip for months and I was intending to splurge, to make this an unforgettable adventure.

"Since I don't need to register, until this evening," I said to Marilyn, "let's spend the day at the pool, OK?" I also had learned, that anytime I needed, I could call for a wheelchair and it would be delivered. This way, I could see the whole picture and not take two hours to get there, by stepping than stopping. The pool was approximately four feet deep, so you could walk through and it was huge!

"Let's see what's in that cave, over there. Hold my arm tighter, Pam."

We walked in the water, entered the cave, and inside was a bar, with stools to sit on, in the actual pool!

"Yep," I said, "this is going to be unforgettable."

"Hey Pam," Marilyn motioned me over to two empty stools. I still had to walk with a cane, but walking in the water without the cane, with the resistance it provided was like, if you fell, oh well.

MAUI WRITERS CONFERENCE

That evening

The conference was amazing! You had access to so many professionals, both in the field of writing novels and screenplays. I had a private meeting with the vice president of the agency which represents the TV show, ER.

I walked up to him, shook his hand and nervously started, "Hi, my name is Pamela and I have an amazing story," I continued to present my ideas, pretty much nonstop, because my time allowance was for only, fifteen minutes,"it's about my being involved in a horrendous accident, comatose for five weeks, with no hope of survival, then waking up to exceed over and above any expectation."

I watched him, as he read my synopsis. He looked up and said, "This sounds like the content for a good movie of the week. When you get back to the Mainland, send me some more of your story, in screenplay form."

"OK and thank you so much," I was just so excited, "it was a pleasure to meet you."

*   *   *

The week had ended and we flew back to the Mainland.

"Now that I'm home, Marilyn, I've got to make this work. Wow, this feels as if my dreams are manifesting."

"They are Pam."

"There's too many of my dreams about to come true, for me to even think about surrendering now. It's as if, I'm being shown just why this all happened to me."

I started climbing the stairs to my bedroom, that was to become, my hangout for some time. And that it did.

* * *

SEPTEMBER 1996

It's night time and I'm upstairs, sitting at my trusty Macintosh, when I hear this strange noise downstairs. It was someone's cat.

"Who are you?" I yelled from the landing. Then, I walked down to pick it up and toss him out the door.

"Come on kitty, you don't live here," I said.

When I picked him up, I lost my balance. Being a warm night, we had the door open and as I was stepping to regain my balance, I ended up outside on the porch.

Next scene is my falling and landing two steps down, but sitting up.

"Help!" I screamed, "Marilyn, I fell!" She ran out, to see me lying on the ground.

"Pam," she screamed, then helped me up and I went right back upstairs to my computer. This time, I sat on a pillow, wedged under one side of my butt, to take pressure off. This was in September of 1996 and by December I thought, I just can't stand this pain anymore. Once again, I needed to go and see the infamous Dr. Garland.

I drove to his office, the next day. "Hey Gar," I hugged him, "long time no see." He looked at me and smiled, "Jansen, what's up?" I described what had happened and he sent me into the x-ray room. When the films were ready, he hung them up, stood there, shaking his head. My spine was curved into an 'S' shape.

"I need to send you in for a CT Scan."

Days later, I returned for the results. Dr. Garland entered and said, "You have a broken back Jansen and one vertebrae has slipped forward on another. We're going to need to schedule you for major back surgery."

On December 9, 1996, I had titanium fused from L-4 to S-1.

Incidentally, I've never heard back about the screenplay, as of yet anyway...

*　*　*

MAY 2007

The phone is ringing as I make my way over to answer it.

"Hello, may I please speak to Pamela?"

"This is Pam."

"Hi Pamela, this is Gwen Hillier, the Associate Casting Director of General Hospital. I'm calling to see if you'd be available for work next Monday the 18th."

"I'd love to," I was trying to sound so calm.

"Now Pam, we start actors off slowly on the show."

After work I ran into Mark Teschner, the head Casting Director and he said to me,

"We'll be having you back. Count on it."

Imagine that, Pamela Jansen on the Soap Opera, General Hospital.

THE END

PAM AND GENERAL HOSPITAL ACTOR
STEVE BURTON

GENERAL HOSPITAL ACTORS

Maurice and Pamela

Jason and Pamela

Ingo and Pamela

Maurice, Pamela and Steve

Pam and Sebastian

Bradford and Pamela

So now I've taken you on a journey
through the life of a somewhat normal
  "Valley Girl" whose life suddenly took
a devastating detour.
    After 25 years of struggle, frustration,
anger, pain, suffering, grief and resentment,
with persistence and faith, I finally arrived
at acceptance.
    I love you Jesus with all my heart!

EPILOGUE

We have all become angry at some point, and maybe said words that hurt and sure there are people that won't forget. We're only human. Remember to get help, forgive yourself, and move on.

Sure our lives have been rearranged. But this isn't an ending. We can channel our energies elsewhere, because there are endless opportunities. There is always going to be that memory of what you were, or what you could have been, but that doesn't exist anymore.

I remember the emotions involved. The frustration and the exhaustion as a result. I also remember that a lot of it came from my inability to accept things. I just had to have things my way, or else. It took years before I finally came to a resolution. I am not claiming to be anger free, at all. I still have moments where I doubt myself and there are times of feeling hopeless. Come on, it's known as being human. I have to stop and tell myself to just get over it. I need to forgive myself and move on.

Acting became a love of mine that, to this day I am not about to shake. Finally discovering my niche in life, I began classes at Media Access, with phenomenal instructors such as, David Zimmerman, Laura Gardner and Christina Kokubo. The program director, Gloria Castaneda and talent development coordinator, Gail Williamson were an outstanding source of support, along with Charles Peterson who was office support for the Media Access Office from the Los Angeles Department of Aging.

I then became involved with Actorsite.com, sitting under an addition of just as phenomenal instructors such as Joan Blair, Kathy Lambdon, Kimberly Crandall, Mark Pinckney, Joe Jeffrey, and the founder of Actorsite Jack Turnbull, a.k.a. JP.

The camaraderie of love, respect, and mutual support is something that I would not trade for a thing. I don't have to look or walk normal because there will always be a character who needs to be portrayed my way.

Another excellent teacher of mine was Diane Christiansen.

One day my photographer, Mary Ann Halpin emailed me to tell me of a book that she was asked to do the photography for, and would I like to be in it? She said that some of the women featured will be, Joni Mitchell, Erin Brokovich, Cybill Shepherd, Joan Lunden, Leeza Gibons, Linda Gray and more to total 50 women.

Let me think for a moment. Now, would I like to be featured in a book with such prominent women?

I am on page 73 of Fearless Women: Midlife Portraits by Nancy Alspaugh and Marilyn Kentz, photography by Mary Ann Halpin.

There is still pain, which I deal with more appropriately, through physical therapy, proper posture, constant reminder from my sister the RN, rather than having a surgery to fix everything that isn't right in my broken body. I know that alternative therapies must be looked at first.

Exercise makes me feel good, even when I'm weary. I'll force myself to get that blood pumping and I become alert. Nutrition is so important for my brain, that I have had to learn the best foods to maintain my energy level. Who am I trying to kid, though? I still love pizza and tacos, but a banana protein drink, and my acai blend will give me what I need in a heart beat.

I stay involved in my interests, acting classes, writing and I enjoy our home in the mountains, with the blue skies and my cat Bosco. Life doesn't get easier, you just get better at it. I still hope to meet that special man who loves the Lord, but at best, now I am more of an emotionally ready person who can be happy alone, or with someone.

MY JEWELRY STAND AT THE LILAC FESTIVAL

ABOUT THE AUTHOR

Over the years, I've come to realize that by confronting depression, I can decide whether to allow it to affect me or not. There are times even today, after all that I've come through and all I've learned, that those moments of sadness try to slow me down. I have to stop and remind myself that time goes by so fast, it's so easy to waste it by dwelling.

I have a free will to be happy and to accomplish my goals. Throughout this time, I've really been brought to an understanding of myself, of people, of love, rejection, the difference between loneliness and being alone.

I truly cherish my quiet time when I sit among the pines and read, or amidst the Poppies, Hollyhocks, Morning Glories, under a soothing sunshine, just relaxing in the early hours of the day.

I am so thankful to be alive now, that one rule I've made is to always take time to enjoy the simple things in life, the beauty in front of me and all around me, which I interpret to mean, always take time to be thankful.

I love you Jesus with all my heart. I sincerely thank you for everything you've done for me.

Here I am speaking at the Disneyland Hotel

Me and my mom, Rosie

Pam at seven years old riding her horse.

Photography by Mary Ann Halpin

ICE SKATES, MY FIRST PAIR

Pam and Dr. Garland thirty years later